Me Myself

by Bob McGrath

Illustrated by Meredith Johnson

PRICE STERN SLOAN
Los Angeles

For his continued good advice, and for taking the time to read and evaluate each story in the Bob's Books series, I would like to thank Dr. Gerald S. Lesser, Professor of Education and Developmental Psychology, Harvard University; Chairman, Board of Advisors, The Children's Television Workshop.

For their sensitive and encouraging input, I would also like to thank the following:

Julia Cummins, Coordinator of Children's Services of the New York Public Library

Dr. Richard Graham, Former Director of the Center for Moral Education and Development at Harvard University

Tom Greening, Ph.D., Editor of the Journal of Humanistic Psychology

Betty Long, Senior Children's Librarian, General Library of the Performing Arts at Lincoln Center (New York Public Library)

Valeria Lovelace, Director of Research - "Sesame Street"

Ann Sperry McGrath, children's book author and preschool teacher

Hannah Nuba, Director of the New York Public Library Early Childhood Resource and Information Center

Lisa Ann Marsoli, Editorial Director — Juvenile Division, Price Stern Sloan

ISBN: 0-8431-2400-8

Library Of Congress Catalog Card Number: 89-30669

10 9 8 7 6 5 4 3 2 1

Guess what? I had a really funny thing happen to me today. I didn't expect anything weird to happen when I got up — I mean, everything seemed the same. Except for one thing, and that was that my brother Timmy didn't wake me up this morning. We usually wrestle on my bed, only today we didn't. I guess he forgot.

I got dressed and did my usual kind of morning stuff: I fed the dog, I had a big bowl of my favorite cereal (and ate it before it got mushy), checked the thermometer outside the kitchen window, grabbed my books, my jacket and cap, and kissed Mom and Dad good-bye.

But before I could get out of the house, my best friend Jerry called and said he was sick and couldn't walk to school with me. I was kind of sorry to hear that, because walking to school with Jerry is usually the best part of my day. We have pretty crazy ideas and really laugh a lot. Yesterday we walked sideways for two blocks.

We pretended that nobody could tell if we were coming or going to school. We got a lot of funny looks, and we were still laughing when we got to school. We laughed so hard, we almost fell over each other. I wonder what we would have thought up today?

I said to my mom, "Heck, Mom, Jerry can't walk to school with me today. That's no fun."

My mom put her arm around me. "I know how you feel. Jerry's your best friend. You'll just have to pretend he's with you today."

But, as it turned out, I didn't have to pretend I was walking to school with Jerry, because when I got to the corner the funny thing I told you about happened. Jerry's cat was waiting for me. At least it looked like he was waiting. He was standing in the exact same place Jerry stands every morning. So I decided if Jerry was sick I might as well walk to school with his cat. It wasn't too far for a cat to walk.

I said, "Hi, Peanutbutter, do you want to walk to school with me today?" It was lucky that I just had breakfast, because every time I'm with Jerry's cat and hear that name, I get hungry.

The cat stood up and began to walk right beside me as if he knew exactly what I had said.

I pretended that Peanutbutter was a real live person and began to think up something funny for us to do on the way to school. First, I began hopping on one foot, but the cat seemed to have trouble doing that. He put back his ears and waved his tail at me. Well, I don't have a tail and I guess he couldn't hop, so I gave up that idea.

Then I began to walk sideways. Jerry would have done that, but I guess it's pretty hard for a cat with four legs. So I said to him, "Let's go backwards, Peanutbutter." Cats are great at backing up, but I guess Peanutbutter wasn't in the mood to do that either.

Finally, I decided it would be easier for me just to pretend we were talking to each other the way I used to make believe I talked to my teddy bear when I was really little. The cat seemed to like that — he stayed right near me. It was funny. It was almost as if he knew I missed Jerry and needed someone to walk to school with. He was right.

First I asked him some questions. People are always pretending that cats have nine lives, so I asked him what it was like to have so many.

I found out right away that talking to Jerry's cat was not at all like talking to Jerry, because Jerry always answers me. Well, almost always. Peanutbutter didn't seem the least bit interested in telling me about his cat lives. He didn't seem the least bit interested in talking to me at all. I guess he just wanted to listen.

"OK," I said, "if you don't want to answer because it's a special cat secret, then I'll tell you about my life." I began to talk about the bike I was hoping to get for my birthday, but as I was talking, Peanutbutter did a strange thing.

He walked ahead of me and sat down right in front of me, blocking my way. When I stopped, he looked up at me and stared at me. I could tell he wanted to hear about something more serious than my birthday. I didn't have to think very hard to find something serious to talk about, because it was right in the middle of my head. But I wondered how he knew about it.

"Well, I guess you found out that I had a fight with my brother Timmy last night, right?"

Peanutbutter didn't move. He looked as if he were waiting for more.

"Well, Timmy changed the channels right in the middle of my favorite TV show. I told him to stop it and he pretended that he didn't hear me. Then I yelled at him to change it back, and he said that my show was boring and he wanted to watch a different show.

"I told him that he changed it right in the middle of the best part and he said that he had already seen it and he told me how it ended. So, I got mad, really mad."

When I got to that part, Peanutbutter flicked his tail. I guess he wanted to hear the whole thing.

"So," I said, "I was really, really mad and somehow we got into a fight. That's when Mom came in, wanting to know what was happening. I blamed everything on Timmy. Mom said she was 'exasperated'.

"Timmy got in trouble for changing the channel and was sent to his room. But before he left, my mom said that if we couldn't watch TV together in peace, we couldn't watch it at all. Then she said, 'No TV for one whole week.'

"Before I went to sleep, Timmy came to the door of my room and said, 'Thanks a lot, kid. You can change the channels on me sometimes and I never get you in trouble.'

"I didn't know what to think about that, because he was right. Sometimes I do it just to tease him, but I always put it back if he gets mad."

Peanutbutter turned his head away. He looked as if he were disappointed in me. "Hey, wait a minute," I said. "Now we can't watch TV for a whole week, so I have a right to be mad, too."

But Peanutbutter stood up and walked towards school without looking back. I followed him and said, "OK, maybe some of it is my fault. If I tease him sometimes, maybe he can tease me sometimes. Maybe I shouldn't have blamed it all on him. But I can't do anything about it now."

We walked side by side. I didn't say anything for awhile, because I was wondering about Timmy. I was wondering why Timmy didn't wake me up and wrestle with me like he always does in the morning.

"Do you think that Timmy is really mad at me?"
I asked. Peanutbutter just kept on walking.
"How about what I did for him last week?"

"Last week I did something really good. I emptied out all the wastepaper baskets even though it was his turn. I put everything into a big plastic bag and left it in his room with a ribbon on it to surprise him and he thought it was great.

"He said I saved him a lot of time and that I was a pretty good younger brother. Mom and Dad took a picture of us together with the plastic bag. When he remembers what I did for him, he can't be mad at me forever."

Peanutbutter just kept on walking and turned into the schoolyard without even waiting for me. He walked up to the school and picked out a cool spot on the cement in the shade. Then he sat down and looked at me. He didn't say anything, but he looked as if he wanted to. I knew he was still listening.

"OK," I said. "I'll meet you here after school and we'll talk some more about Timmy. Maybe I should tell him I'm sorry about the fight. Maybe I should tell him that I won't change the channels on him anymore. Maybe I'll tell him I won't tease him anymore."

Peanutbutter laid down and rested his head on his front paws. It looked as if he was going to wait all day. I knew he would be all right because I'd seen him hanging around the school lots of times.

And sure enough, when school was over, there he was ready to listen to me again. It was really funny walking to school with a cat. Even though cats can't talk, I think they like to listen. Talking to a cat is kind of like hearing yourself saying things.

Who knows, maybe from now on it will be me, Jerry and Peanutbutter all walking to school together.